What's different about the United Methodist Church?

Bishop
BRUCE P. BLAKE

Hymns by Charles Wesley are from the United Methodist Hymnal.
Used by permission.

*Dedicated to the lay persons of
The United Methodist Church
from whom I have learned that
the essence of United Methodist Witness
is how we practice our faith.*

Contents

Acknowledgments

This material was first presented at the 1997 Session of the Oklahoma Conference of The United Methodist Church to explore what I am convinced is the missing component in the search for renewal and vitality in The United Methodist Church in America.

Many persons have explored the beliefs of United Methodist Christians. This is essential! Many persons have explored the polity of The United Methodist Church. This is essential. In response to these explorations changes have been considered and made in both United Methodist beliefs and polity. However, these changes have not been the source or impetus for renewal.

It is my opinion that the reason for this is that even though our beliefs and polity are the source of our distinctiveness, our distinctiveness is discovered and experienced in our character, the way we live together, the practice of our faith. I choose to refer to this as the ethos of The United Methodist Church.

Ethos is a behavioral word. The word translated "ethos" is the same root word of "ethic." The exploration of ethos is an examination of our ethic, our behavior as United Methodists. In Wesley's words, our ethos is "experimental and practical divinity." The Methodist movement was first distinctive within the Church of England, not only because of belief and/or polity, but because of this experimental and practical divinity of people called Methodists.

In the opening "conversation" of the conference held June 25, 1744, three themes were addressed: first, how to regulate our doctrine; second, how to regulate our discipline; third, how to regulate our practice. The practice of faith is our ethos!

When United Methodists are not distinctive, it is because we have neglected and/or lost our ethos. Ethos cannot be separated from doctrine. Doctrine offers normative guidelines for ethos. What I am urging is that in seminaries and in local churches we change the subject of our studies from "United Methodist Doctrine and Polity" to "United Methodist Doctrine, Ethos and Polity."

I am indebted to the United Methodist Churches in Angola, Liberia, Zimbabwe, and the Philippines for allowing me to visit and experience the vitality and renewal of The United Methodists in those countries. The story of faithfulness of the United Methodist witness in these countries is awesome and inspiring to me. In each case the cornerstone of this faithfulness is their practice of the faith, their ethos.

These experiences outside the United States have convinced me that the history of the Methodist movement in the U. S. has been weakened by our lack of attention to ethos. There are many denominations in the United States which separated from the Methodist Church. Why? Not just because of doctrine and polity, but rather because of practice, ethos.

I am also indebted to the local congregations I have been privileged to observe in the Kansas West, North Texas, Oklahoma, and Oklahoma Indian Missionary Conferences which are constantly renewed and faithful. Every single one of these is distinctive, not just because of beliefs or polity, but because of ethos, their practice of the faith.

These congregations have convinced me that movements within the denomination today would not be as attractive if our whole denomination would recapture our essential ethos. In these vital congregations these movements never get a hearing because these movements are based on critique of a weakened ethos. Where ethos is clear such movements are null and void.

The invitation of Jesus Christ was "to follow me." To follow Jesus is not simply how we believe and how we are organized. It has to do with discipleship and discipleship is a matter of practice, a matter of ethos.

In 1996 The General Conference affirmed that the purpose

of The United Methodist Church, global and local, is to make disciples. Making disciples is more than a set of beliefs and an organizational strategy. Making disciples has to do with ethics and practice, our ethos!

This material is organized into three sections. The first section, "What Makes Us Tick," explores three components of our ethos which are the basic ingredients of the United Methodist practice of faith. The second section, "The Magnets of Our Ethos," explores three components of our ethos which are attractive. These offer what persons are searching for today. The third section, "Launched Into God's Future," explores three components of our ethos which propel United Methodists out of our past into God's future.

Following the exploration of each of these nine components, there are discussion starter questions for study groups, church school classes, and other units of the church who use these materials.

Finally, I am indebted to Dr. Boyce Bowdon and Dr. David Severe and Rev. Grayson Lucky, who have been instrumental in the preparation of this book. Without their encouragement and assistance this project would not have occurred.

Section One:

What Makes the United Methodist Church Tick?

Chapter 1

United Methodists Lead With Grace, Not With Judgment

In this first section I will explore three components of the United Methodist ethos (practice of the faith) which have brought to this denomination a distinctiveness which has been consistent through the generations.

In our home we have a clock that sets on our mantle. It's been passed through four generations of my family. When we forget to wind it, the pendulum stops. It's nice to look at but it doesn't keep time. It doesn't tick. It is simply a piece of furniture. However, when it is wound it keeps perfect time. These components of our ethos are what wind us up and makes us tick as United Methodists.

First, and basic to the ethic, the behavior of being a Methodist and now a United Methodist, is that in our ethos we lead with grace, not judgment.

This is a consistent theme in the life and teachings of Jesus. In John 8:1-11 the story is told of the woman who was caught in adultery? The scribes and the Pharisees—hoping to trap Jesus—brought her before Jesus and reminded him that the law of Moses gave her accusers the right to stone her to death. "What do you say?" they asked. Jesus stooped over and doodled in the sand. Finally he said to them, "Let anyone among you who is without sin be the first to throw a stone at her."

This is what it means to lead with grace and not judgment!

Among United Methodists this component of our corporate and individual behavior is rooted in our belief about God. We believe leading with grace is God's inclination towards humankind as revealed in Jesus Christ. This belief about God determines the controversial way we behave the doctrine of grace - the way we live it out. Wesley compiled his "controversial" writings. He included his sermon on "Free Grace," which ended his collegial relationship with George Whitfield. This ethic of free grace is our distinctiveness, i.e. we lead with grace, not judgment. This simply means that the United Methodist practice of faith does not lead us to ask the question, "Who is my neighbor?" Rather the question is, "Who isn't my neighbor?"

This is true in relationship to other denominations. We are truly catholic and universal in our attitude towards other denominations. We are partners in Christ with them rather than competing against them. This is not just a matter of legislation that can be changed by an act of the General Conference. This is a constitutional matter in The United Methodist Church.

Fifteen years ago I preached a series of 13 sermons on the Book of Revelation. My goal was to counter the reality that most church members either take this book literally as a forecast of the 20th century or totally disregard it. Every Sunday I prepared a bulletin insert interpreting the scripture. Another pastor in town became so upset with my attempt to interpret Revelation in a non-literal fashion that he sent a lay person to pick up the bulletin insert at our 8:30 service and tape my sermon. The pastor would listen to the tape of my sermon and at his 11:00 a.m. service he preached against my interpretation.

The ethical (ethos) issue was that he was non-ecumenical in his behavior and attitude. United Methodists do not preach against the teachings of another church because we lead with grace, not judgment.

United Methodists also lead with grace, not judgment, in relationship to individuals. We are clear: persons are equal in that all are in need of God's grace and therefore stand in need of the ministry of the church. This is a matter of ethics. The fact that I know I am a sinner mandates that I accept every other person as a sinner. This prevents me from judging another as one whose sin is greater than mine. This is the reason that on the controversial subject of gay and lesbian persons participating in the life of the church the distinctive United Methodist position is that we welcome these persons into the life of the church. We also have standards. For example, we do not perform holy unions between gay and lesbian persons. However, these standards are in the context of grace; we welcome every person to the community of Christ and the table of the church.

There are many illustrations that we lead with grace not judgment. Grace is not a distinct doctrine; many non-United Methodists affirm this doctrine. However, for United Methodists it is a determinative doctrine. It determines our practice, the way we relate to other denominations and every person as a child of God! If this is not clear in every single United Methodist local congregation, we have failed in representing our distinctive United Methodist ethos in that community that we lead with grace, not judgment.

No one put it better than Charles Wesley in a hymn that we do not often sing: "Blow Ye the Trumpet, Blow."

1. "Blow ye the trumpet, blow! The gladly solemn sound let all the nations know, to earth's remotest bound:

2. Jesus, our great high priest, hath full atonement made; ye weary spirits, rest; ye mournful souls, be glad:

5. Ye who have sold for nought your heritage above shall have it back unbought, the gift of Jesus' love:

6. The gospel trumpet hear, the news of heavenly grace; and saved from earth, appear before your Savior's face"

Chorus:

The year of jubilee is come! The year of jubilee is come! Return, ye ransomed sinners, home.

Questions for Discussion

- In your personal journey of faith, where have there been those occasions when you were able to lead with grace, not judgment?
- What have been those occasions when you found it most difficult to lead with grace?
- Over the years there have been individuals and groups of persons who have experienced the judgment of the church long before they heard the message of God's grace. What are some notable examples of these in your memory?
- In what ways would the life of your local church become different if this grace-first component of United Methodist ethos prevailed in your life together?

Chapter 2

United Methodists
Are A Sent People

Our 200 year history has been distinctive in the understanding that United Methodists are a sent people. This is rooted in our belief in the witness of the Spirit through those who are sent.

There are many references in the Bible to this component of our ethos. Matthew 10 is a chapter on the "sent ministry" of the disciples.

"These twelve Jesus sent out..." (Matthew 10: 5); "Behold, I send you out like sheep in the midst of wolves; therefore be shrewd as serpents, and innocent as doves" (Matthew 10:16).

One who has not been called by God cannot answer, and those who have not answered cannot be sent.

This is true in relationship to clergy who are sent by the conference where their membership is held to serve in a particular place. The bishop is the agent of the church who appoints pastors—sends pastors—to their place of service.

I recently visited with a pastor who had been given permission to choose where he would serve. There was a group of persons who withdrew from the congregation. This pastor was carrying a great deal of anxiety and guilt, for he believed he was fully responsible and accountable for the departure of these persons. Whether these persons left as a consequence of his leadership is not the issue I want to raise. The issue is that this pastor chose to serve in that place and therefore stood alone in feeling fully responsible and accountable for what had happened.

If the pastor had been sent to serve, the whole annual conference and its superintendents could have stood with the pastor and the church in exploring what was happening according to the standards of faith and the purpose of the church. The sent ministry is a corporate act of a corporate people. When a pastor or a bishop is sent to a place to serve, each brings the strength of the corporate community including standards, prayers, and experience. Whereas, when one chooses to serve in a particular place, one finally stands alone and is often lonely.

United Methodist clergy are a sent people and this is our distinctiveness. It is not that United Methodist clergy have skills that distinguish them from other pastors in a community. What sets United Methodist clergy apart is that we are sent to serve a community through a local congregation.

Sent ministry is also the experience of United Methodist lay persons. Today the popular notion is that persons are involved in the church on the basis of "what they get out of it." Church involvement has become normed by consumerism, "I will shop until I find a church that fills my needs." And often these shoppers shop until they drop. This is not the ethic/ethos of The United Methodist Church. One of the basic needs of human beings is to give. Therefore, laity are the people of God who are sent by the corporate community into the world to give of themselves, to serve.

The United Methodist Church does not exist for the sake of itself. It exists for the sake of others. This is one of the exciting dimensions of the new order of deacons in the church. This is a new order. It is not the same as elders experienced as they were first ordained deacon. It is a new order. One of the basic standards of the deacon is that their work, if it is primarily in the community of faith, must be directly and intentionally related to witness in the world. The deacon is to lead all elders and lay persons in understanding the inseparable relationship between work and worship, between the gathered community and the scattered serving community.

The reason why United Methodists worship is to declare the worth of God and in so doing be aware of God's mission in the world. John 3:16 does not say God loved the church so much he gave his only son. It says God loved the world so much that he gave his only son. We are to be reminded of this when we depart to serve. The reason why United Methodists learn in study experiences in the church is to be more faithful servants at home, work, school and play.

United Methodists are the sent people. This is in the biblical tradition of the story of the early church, the Acts of the Apostles. Apostles are the "sent ones." United Methodists are the sent people!

Through the new Episcopal Initiative, "Children and Poverty," Bishops of the Church are calling every congregation and every United Methodist to create a circle of care around every child in every community. It is the responsibility of the church to be certain that children who are affluent have a Christian home, not just a house in which to dwell, food to eat, and playthings to entertain. It is the responsibility of the church to be certain that children who are poor have a Christian home in which there is basic food and shelter to enable them to experience love.

The foundational understanding of this Initiative is that United Methodists are a sent people. Basic to the United Methodist practice of the faith is that we are the sent people. If this is not clear in every single United Methodist local congregation, we have failed in representing our distinctive United Methodist ethos in that community. United Methodists not only lead with grace, we are the sent people and we behave that way.

This is expressed clearly in the hymn, "Forth in Thy Name, O Lord" by Charles Wesley:
  1. "Forth in thy name, O Lord, I go, my daily labor to pursue; thee, only thee, resolved to know in all I think or speak or do.
  2. The task thy wisdom hath assigned, O let me cheerfully fulfill; in all my works thy presence

find, and prove thy good and perfect will.

3. Thee may I set at my right hand, whose eyes mine inmost substance see, and labor on at thy command, and offer all my works to thee."

Questions for Discussion

- Where has the message of the gospel and the cry of God's people "sent" you into service and ministry in your life time?
- Where have you felt sent, didn't want to go, but experienced grace in obedience, and joy in service?
- Think of the pastors who have been sent to your congregation over the years. List and share with someone else the gifts which you think each brought to your church, or to you personally.
- In your life journey how has your concept of the role of a pastor changed? Do you agree that when pastors are sent that there is a greater sense of the corporate backing of the pastor and the congregation at work? If so, how? If not, why?
- At the conclusion of worship service or study groups, do you have the feeling of being sent into God's world to serve? If so, what difference has that made in your Christian life-style? If you do not experience this kind of "being sent," would you be open to being challenged and sent to serve at the conclusion of worship or study?

Chapter 3

United Methodists Minister With The Poor

For the past 200 years, the United Methodist ethic/ ethos has had its very core ministry with the poor. This characteristic of our ethos is one of the best illustrations of the reality that we cannot discover the soul of the Methodist movement by only exploring the beliefs and polity of the church. Ministry with the poor is not just a belief system or an organizational principle. Ministry with the poor is a matter of behavior, a matter of ethics, a matter of ethos!

The biblical witness of James 2 makes this clear: "My friends, show no partiality as you hold the faith of our Lord Jesus Christ, the Lord of glory." Friends, this gets more difficult for us United Methodists. "For if a person with gold rings and in fine clothing comes into your assembly, and a poor man in shabby cloth also comes in, and you pay attention to the one who wears fine clothing and say, 'Have a seat here, please,' while you say to the poor man, 'Stand there,' or, 'Sit at my feet,' have you not made distinctions among yourselves and become judges with evil thoughts?"

John Wesley, the founder of the Methodist movement within the Church of England, often is remembered for his experience in 1738 when he went to a class meeting and his "heart was strangely warmed." We remember this, for when a hard-hearted, hard-driving young zealot and disciplinarian all of a sudden discovered the warmth of love which lead to a whole different understanding of Christian discipleship. This a remarkable and romantic story of faith called Aldersgate.

However, it must be noted that Wesley seldom referred to this experience in his own journal or sermons. The turning point for Wesley was that in 1739, a year later, he started preaching out of doors, on the lawn, on the green, in public places. Why? Because he was driven by a conviction that only as Christians were involved with a ministry with the poor can the church be faithful followers of Christ. Wesley referred to Newgate more than Aldersgate. Newgate was where he practiced ministry with those in prison.

Wesley's commitment to the poor is represented in hymns, many of which are not common in the United States. It is interesting to note that most of these are in hymnologies of the Great Britain church, and not in the United States churches. In the United States we have shunned these references to the poor in Wesley hymns. Charles Wesley's hymn, "Jesus a Gift Divine I Know," is one of these hymns. The words are a striking testimony of John and Charles Wesley's commitment.

> "On mercy's wings I swiftly fly
> The poor and helpless to relieve,
> My life, my all, for them to give."

John Wesley was a student of the Bible. I challenge anyone to read the biblical witness and reach any other conclusion than Wesley reached, i.e. to be a faithful follower of Christ one must be involved in ministry with the poor. This is not just a matter of choice; this is the imperative of the One who "became poor" for our sake!

Since Wesley, the movement has made this clear. The Methodist movement was a key to the late nineteenth century movement, the Sunday school. The purpose of the Sunday school was not to teach already committed Christians and their children. The original purpose of the Sunday school was to reach the children of poverty in the cities!

This is the reason why, along with local churches, the Methodist movement has always had institutional and agency expressions of ministry. What makes these institutions and agencies part of The United Methodist Church is not an organizational relationship. Often what makes them United Methodist is their commitment to a ministry with the poor. It is tragic that too often local churches have left this expression of our ethos to our agencies and institutions. Ministry with the poor is not an option for The United Methodist Church. The biblical witness does not exempt local congregations from the practice of ministry with the poor.

One of my personal learnings has been that ministry *to* the poor is not the foundation of the United Methodist ethos. Rather the foundation of the United Methodist ethos is ministry *of* the poor. The poor have much to offer me. They are usually far more faithful than I am. They teach me that in God's reign there are no classes, dress codes or monetary advantages. I am personally convinced every Christian who is caught up in materialism and consumerism, which includes Bruce Blake, stands in need of the ministry of the poor. Only when I am willing to be ministered unto do I have the right to minister to others.

The cornerstone of ministry with the poor is not ministry *to* the poor—it is ministry *of* the poor. This is the United Methodist witness and this component of our ethos makes the local United Methodists distinctive in every community.

Charles Wesley stated this so clearly in the hymn, "Come Sinners to the Gospel Feast."

1. Come, sinners, to the gospel feast; let every soul be Jesus' guest. Ye need not one be left behind, for God had bid all human kind.
2. Sent by my Lord, on you I call the invitation is to all. Come, all the world! Come, sinner, thou! All things in Christ are ready now.
3. Come, all ye souls by sin oppressed, ye restless wanderers after rest; ye poor, and maimed, and halt, and blind, in Christ a hearty welcome find.

Questions for Discussion

- On what occasions have you been ministered to by a person who understands themselves to be poor?
- What gifts do those who are poor have to give which cannot be given by others?
- Think for a moment about your deepest feelings regarding the poor in our society. How do you view them? What part of your feelings and attitudes are borne out of the Bible witness about the poor, and what part is informed by political or social viewpoints? How might you change if you took more of the biblical view over against the political or social?
- What ministries are present in and through your church that relate directly to the poor in your community? What new ways could you see that would relate you more di rectly in a ministry with those and of those who are poor in your community?
- What barriers in your local church prevent involvement of the poor? How might those barriers be addressed through a "grace-first" attitude in your congregation?

Summary of Section One:
What Makes Us Tick?

There are three historic ingredients of the United Methodist ethos which are basic to our identity and life-style. They are what make us tick. First, we lead with grace, not judgment. Second, we are the people sent to serve. Third, ministry with the poor is based on the ministry of the poor. Only as these three are apparent in every United Methodist agency/institution and local congregation are we faithful to the distinctive United Methodist witness!

If these are not clear in every single United Methodist local congregation, we have failed in representing our distinctive United Methodist ethos in the community.

When a person sees United Methodist ministry and mission, do they see a church, agency or institution which leads with grace, not judgment, people who are sent to serve and who are committed to a ministry with the poor? Are we ticking?

If not, we are not faithful; we are, as the clock, simply nice to look at, a piece of furniture. If we are ticking, we accept these high standards which are our calling to fulfill!

Questions for Discussion

- What are the signs of "ticking," being alive, keeping time with God's missions in God's world, in your congregation?
- What are the signs of your local church standing still, not "ticking," without movement?
- What one to three things, if done well, would be the most likely activities to begin your church's journey toward a preferred future as understood by our United Methodist ethos?

Section Two:

The Magnets of Our Ethos

Chapter 4

United Methodists
Live In Community

In the first section we explored three historic ingredients of the United Methodist ethos. These three, though, are not all inclusive of our ethos. In this section I will explore three additional components which are historic but have an additional quality which makes them important today.

The best way to describe this quality is to share that as a child one of my favorite toys was my father's magnet. It was shaped like a horseshoe, about 3/4 of an inch thick, and really powerful. The best thing about it was that I could spill all the thumbtacks and clips from my father's desk on the kitchen floor. I could move the magnet around and the tacks and clips would be attracted and attached to the magnet. Attract - zap - attach—that was the rhythm of my game.

This is the image I want to explore with you in this section. There are, in my judgment, three components of our ethos/ethic which will attract , zap and attach persons to The United Methodist Church today because these three intersect a deep yearning in the lives of people in this decade!

The first of these magnetic components is that the United Methodist life-style is one which insists that faith development occurs in the community of faith.

Scripture abounds with texts which affirm that faith development occurs in the community of faith. For example, consider this passage from the Book of Acts, chapter two, verses 43-47.

"And everyone kept feeling a sense of awe; and many wonders and signs were taking place through the apostles.

And all those who had believed were together, and had all things in common; and they began selling their property and possessions, and were sharing them with all, as anyone might have need. And day by day continuing with one mind in the temple, and breaking bread from house to house, they were taking their meals together with gladness and sincerity of heart, praising God, and having favor with all the people. And the Lord was adding to their number day by day those who were being saved."

As United Methodists we take seriously the story of the early church. What characterized a person as a Christian early in the life of the church was not only a particular set of beliefs, but that an individual was part of a community which was known as Christian. The standards of Wesley's disciplined life insisted on involvement in a class meeting where a person's life could be continually strengthened by others who inquired, among other questions, "How is your soul?" Today, the question of every United Methodist is, "Will you support the church with your prayers, gifts, service and presence?" We insist that to be a Christian one must be present in a community of faith.

The introductory words to each of the three general rules of our tradition are "continuing to give evidence." To be a United Methodist is to continue to give evidence of faith. This is the cornerstone of the practice of accountability within the community of faith.

Tragically, many clergy and lay persons are exempt from any discernible accountability for their discipleship today. We have so individualized Christianity in the United States that we have generally ignored this necessary ingredient of the Christian faith.

A friend from Africa visited the United States. He was not educated here, but has visited several times. I asked him about the difference between the United Methodist experience of the faith in the United States and in his home country. He said, "You sing 'I songs,' and we sing 'we songs.'" For a person who doesn't know English well, he made his point. We have ignored Christian accountability in the faith because of this concentration on individuality. As a consequence many clergy and laity are exempt from any discernible accountability for discipleship.

Many proclaim that to be a Christian is solely dependent on a person's relationship to God. This reflects the individualization and privatization of life in the western part of God's world, particularly the United States. The United Methodist ethos is that a person can be a believer on their own as an unrelated individual. However to be a Christian one must be part of a community of faith. This practice does not deal with the question of salvation at the event of death which is God's judgment call. What it has to do with is a particular and distinctive United Methodist ethic that to be a Christian one must be in a community of faith with other Christians where together persons pray, support each other, and from which they are sent forth to serve.

If we would raise this component of our life-style to the visibility of all to see, it would be as a magnet—zapping, attracting and attaching people, because people to day are lonely, isolated and hungry for the meaningful relationships possible in a Christian community governed by the gifts of the spirit, kindness, patience, gentleness and self-control. The world is starved for such a community and the United Methodist ethos insists on these standards. Christian community is not just a fellowship where persons are nice and polite to each other. This is God's community in which we love one another. It is an inclusive community where every person is not only welcomed but loved. It is not a community which exists for its own sake. It is a community of corporate servanthood.

This component of our ethos is particularly attractive to Generation Xers. My challenge is to observe a local congregation. If there are no Generation Xers present, one of the reasons is because the community of faith is not apparent to these persons as an inclusive and accountable

community of God's love where the gifts of the spirit abound!
No one put it better than Charles Wesley in his hymn,
"Blest Be the Dear Uniting Love:"

1. "Blest be the dear uniting love that will not let us
   part; our bodies may far off remove, we still are
   one in heart.
2. Joined in one spirit to our Head, where he appoints
   we go, and still in Jesus' footsteps tread, and do his
   work below.
4. We all are one who him receive, and each with each
   agree, in him the One, the Truth, we live; blest point
   of unity!
5. Partakers of the Savior's grace, and same in mind
   and heart, nor joy, nor grief, nor time, nor place,
   nor life, nor death can part."

Questions for Discussion

- What is your earliest recollection of being aware that as a Christian you were part of a community of faith, rather than just an individual person of faith?
- When, in your personal journey of faith, have you tried to be a believer apart from an active participation in a community of faith?
- Share with at least one other person a time or times when you were sustained and lifted up by knowing the joy of being in a community of faithful people.
- Does the congregation in which you participate express more of an "I" or a "we" Christianity? What would be helpful in developing more of a "we" understanding?
- Share a time when you were held accountable or when you were part of holding another person accountable for their faith. Did you experience that event as positive or negative to the life of the community of faith? If you have not had these experiences, why do you think you haven't, and do you think it would help you in your Christian journey to have a greater level of accountability for living out your faith?

Chapter 5

United Methodists Practice Education Without Indoctrination

The second magnet which will zap, attract, and attach persons to the United Methodist witness is that we experience education without indoctrination. This is a distinctive emphasis today.

In a world marked by insecurity, many persons naturally are inclined towards doctrinaire styles of life where answers are clear and definite. The most insightful article I read about the 39 members of Heaven's Gate, who in March of 1997, committed suicide as a fulfillment of their life together in a cult emphasized that this group was certain they had the answers.

I am personally convinced that a murder is occurring in the world today. The victim is reason. Reason is being murdered in the Information Age. Education has become equated with information rather than reason. I am also convinced this is not God's will. Jesus taught, "You shall love the Lord your God with all your heart, and with all your soul, and with all your mind" (Matthew 22:34-38). To love God with our mind mandates that we reason together!

Wesley began his movement in the context of persons being certain they had answers. In the 19th century answers were clear and definite. Salvation was based on being theologically correct. The priests of the church kept the laity from inquiring about their beliefs by providing answers, oftentimes to questions they were not asking. To counter this practice, Wesley established the Christian library for all participants in the class meeting. The books of this library included classics as well as devotional material. The authors of these books did not agree with each other because Wesley did not affirm the necessity of Methodists agreeing with one another. He wanted Methodists to be educated, with the ability to think for themselves, rather than be indoctrinated in a way that eliminated critical thinking. From the beginning, the Methodist movement was one of education without indoctrination.

Jesus emphasized that one must love God with one's mind. There is no conflict between mental development and faith. Jesus was a person who raised provocative questions. Christianity, according to the United Methodist ethos, is a journey of inquiry, not a discovery of answers.

This is the reason why United Methodists have been committed to the church being part of higher education. A college or university does not have to leave The United Methodist Church in order to be free to inquire in any field of study. This is the reason we started the first private university on the continent of Africa. The United Methodist Church wants every person to have freedom of thought that leads to freedom of people. A scholar in a United Methodist college and university is often more free to inquire than in most public or private universities because The United Methodist Church affirms the value of education without indoctrination.

I was with a youth group about a year ago. We talked about why the church was important in that community. While we talked about this issue, tears started streaming out of the high school junior's eyes. I asked, "What's going on. This isn't a tear-jerker is it?" She responded. "I just realized that every time I express a thought at home I'm corrected. At school every time I express my thoughts I'm corrected. This is the only place where I can express my thoughts and be accepted." This local church knows what education without indoctrination is all about.

This book is not about beliefs or polity. However, I do want to note that our life-style of education without indoctrination does not imply that United Methodists can believe anything we want to believe. There are standards, parameters of belief, with scripture being the most determinative. What our ethos affirms is that whether one is within those standards and parameters is finally the choice and decision of the individual.

The practice of education without indoctrination has two clear consequences in our life together. First, The United Methodist Church as a group cannot think. The United Methodist Church does not have a brain. Individuals, not groups, have brains. Therefore, when the church acts, it is by a majority vote or consensus of human beings who may be right or wrong because it is a process whereby human beings are seeking to determine God's will. Whether the church is right or wrong is God's call, not the church's claim.

The second consequence is that as United Methodists we disagree with each other. We believe that truth more likely will emerge out of disagreement than when a doctrine is established and taught without the privilege of it being examined or questioned.

The Christian movement was born in the cradle of disagreement. Consider the disagreement between Peter and Paul as described in the Acts of the Apostles. United Methodists are comfortable with this tradition of the church because we experience education without indoctrination.

As my father, an immigrant from Scotland, shared with me, "Bruce, as long as you agree with 51% of the laws of America you must support all of them and work to change the 49%. If you ever agree with less than 50% you need to find another country." So it is with the church. As long as United Methodists agree with 51% of the decisions of its representative leadership, we give 100% support and work to change the 49%. When we agree with less than 50%, we need to find another church home. United Methodists are never expected to agree with the church 100% because every United Methodist has a brain and is encouraged to use it.

There are millions of persons in the United States who have said "No" to the church because they believe all Christian churches try to indoctrinate members and prevent them from thinking for themselves. They do not know of our distinctive ethos of education without indoctrination. If they could clearly see this they would be drawn to the United Methodist witness. They would be attracted, zapped and attached to a church which affirms their right to think and inquire about all things, for we experience education without indoctrination.

Charles Wesley represents this expression of United Methodist ethos in the hymn, "Spirit of Faith, Come Down,"

1. "Spirit of faith, come down, reveal the things of God; and make to us the God-head known, and witness with the blood.

"Tis thine the blood to apply and give us eyes to see, who did for every sinner die hath surely died for me.

4. Inspire the living faith (which whosoever receive, the witness in themselves they have and consciously believe), the faith that conquers all, and doth the mountain move, and saves whoe'er on Jesus call, and perfects them in love."

Questions for Discussion

- In your personal journey of faith, when did you first begin to realize that you were free to think for yourself, and that your church was not going to do your thinking for you?
- What controversial issues are you uncomfortable or un willing to address, think about, discuss? Thinking back over your life, were there other issues you once were reluctant to discuss, but are now open to thoughtful consideration?
- On a scale of 1-10, with 10 being education and 1 being indoctrination, where would you place your church in the worship/preaching area, and in the education/teaching area? Do you sense that this position has expressed an open welcome, or a feeling of exclusion to those who might not agree with the position taken?
- What stories of open disagreement in the life of your local congregation can you tell? When was there a time of avoiding the disagreements present in the congregation? What were the consequences of each for the life of the congregation?
- What current controversial issues, present in our society, should be discussed openly and creatively in your congregation, Sunday School class, or other groups? Should the pastor be encouraged to preach sermons dealing with these issues? Why?

Chapter 6

United Methodists
Are A Connecting People

The third component which attracts, zaps and attaches persons to the United Methodist Church is the component of connection.

The connection is under severe critique by many today. It is interesting that when I explore our ethos from a biblical perspective, I find many references to Christians being connected.

Jesus said, "And if a kingdom is divided against itself, that kingdom cannot stand. And if a house is divided against itself, that house will not be able to stand" (Mark 3:24-25). One of the very best illustrations is that very familiar parable in John 15: "I am the true vine, and My Father is the vinedresser. Every branch in Me that does not bear fruit, He takes away...I am the vine, you are the branches." The point of the text is that once a branch is split from the vine it's no longer connected.

Paul's first letter to the church at Corinth has a tremendous 12th chapter on connection. "For even as the body is one and yet has many members, and all the members of the body, though they are many, are one body, so also is Christ" (Corinthians 12:12).

He had to hammer away at this for this theme is found throughout Paul's letters. In his letter to the Thessalonians, he wrote, "But we request of you, brethren, that you appreciate those who diligently labor among you, and have charge over you in the Lord and give you instruction, and that you esteem them very highly in love because of their work. Live in peace with one another" (Thessalonians 5:12-13). And he continues to explore what Christian conduct is as we are connected to each other.

For the past decade in our culture networking has become the "in" word in many fields of activity. Computers have become networked. Persons who have similar interests have become networked. Companies which have similar production and distribution needs have become networked. The epitome of networking is the Internet on which persons and groups throughout the world communicate and are in touch with each other.

This phenomenon, my friends, is not just driven by technology and economic profit. The bottom line is not economic. The bottom line is that our society has developed into a culture of dependency on distance rather than intimacy. For many persons, the most intimate experience in life happens as they watch television. The opportunity to be in mutual relationships are few and far between.

A 75-year-old farmer said to me in 1965, "You know, Bruce, two things are really hurting our community: TV and air conditioning. It used to be when it was too hot to be inside we were outside visiting with neighbors and friends. Now we are all inside staying cool with air conditioning. It used to be when families and friends were with each other we would visit, play cards and games. Now we sit next to each other and watch TV." Clarence was right. Thirty-five years later we have accepted the reality that distance rather than intimacy is our way of life.

Networking is one of the counter movements against this phenomenon. The reason why this observation is appropriate to the consideration of United Methodist ethos is that networking has been and is a distinctive part of the United Methodist ethos. We simply have called it by a different name. We call it the United Methodist connection. Every principle that is heralded as networking today is, in fact, an historic principle of the United Methodist connection.

When we examine our life-style of connecting we discover that we do not allow clergy to exist as independent and individualistic entrepreneurs. Clergy are connected to each other by having their church membership in the conference. This is where our commitment of prayers, presence, gifts and service are shared. The exciting expression of this was adopted in the General Conference of 1996 as all clergy, deacons and elders will become part of orders which are responsible for developing the commitment of prayers, presence, gifts and service of deacons and elders with each other.

We do not allow laity to live out their journey of faith in isolation from other Christians. The United Methodist standards of church membership insist on Christians being in relationship to each other, not only in relationship with God.

We do not allow congregations to be independent of each other. Every congregation is part of a district and a conference. This horizontal connection, networking, is a genius of the United Methodist life-style.

I am amused when persons complain about our connection but affirm networking in every other way. Recently I was criticized and condemned for being an advocate of the United Methodist connection by a person who is significantly involved in fantasy baseball and football. When I pointed out to him the hypocrisy in affirming network ing in athletics, because he did not want to be an isolated fan for he wants to be in relationship to other fans, while at the same time criticizing the church for affirming the same principle our discussion moved to a significantly different level.

Millions of persons in our culture have had their gas tanks run empty on distance, individualism and independence. They are seeking to be connected! If our pews are not full on Sunday morning, it just might be that we have not raised the flag of the United Methodist connection for all to see. It just might be we do not have a flag to unfurl! I asked an 80-year-old woman why she and six others continued to be the faithful church in their community. She responded, "How else could we build Africa University?" This and many other examples illustrate the thrill and excitement of United Methodists networking. This is the excitement and thrill that youth are seeking in gangs, adults in cults, and all persons in a variety of ways.

Instead of putting our light of connecting under a basket, hidden from all, we need to put it on a hilltop for all to see, for when they see us as a networking people, they will be attracted - zapped and attached to the United Methodist witness.

Charles Wesley expressed this connection in the hymn, "Jesus, United by Thy Grace,"

1. "Jesus, united by thy grace and each to each endeared, with confidence we seek thy face and know our prayer is heard.

2. Help us to help each other, Lord, each other's cross to bear; let all their friendly aid afford, and feel each other's care.

3. Up unto thee, our living Head, let us in all things grow; till thou hast made us free indeed and spotless here below.

4. Touched by the lodestone of thy love, let all our hearts agree, and ever toward each other move, and ever move toward thee."

Questions for Discussion

- Make a list of all the kinds of networks in which you participate in your life.
- When you look at the ministries of The United Methodist Church made possible by our being connected, working together, which ones are you most excited about?
- Where do you see needs in your community, or elsewhere, that could be best met by our connecting together as churches to make a difference, where we are not now working?

Summary of Section Two:
The Magnets of Our Ethos?

In summary, the United Methodist ethos and practice will attract, zap and attach persons as steel to a magnet as these components of community, education without indoctrination, and connection are evident for all to see.

If we, in every local church, fail to live this out in our life together, we will repel others who are starved for community, education without indoctrination, and connection.

On the other hand, when these are evident, these same persons who otherwise will be repelled will be attracted to the distinctive United Methodist witness. These are the tools for the evangelistic task.

It has been said that the evangelistic task is one beggar telling another beggar where to find food. It is my opinion, my friends, that persons are begging for what we offer. The question is, "Do we care enough to tell them where to find food?"

Questions for Discussion

- Where in your local church have you seen people attracted, zapped and attached to your life in faith together?
- What were the magnetic attractive forces that drew you to the congregation you now attend?
- In what ways do you feel your church may have become less attractive to new people? What might it do to change this?

Section Three:

Launching Into God's Future

Chapter 7

United Methodists Grow and Change

In section one of this consideration of United Methodist ethos, we explored three components of our practice of faith which are historic and crucial to our identity:

1) United Methodists lead with grace—not judgment;
2) United Methodists are a sent people;
3) United Methodists are in ministry with the poor.

In part two we explored three components which will attract, zap, and attach persons to the United Methodist witness as steel to a magnet:

1) United Methodists live in Christian community;
2) United Methodists experience education without indoctrination;
3) United Methodists are a connected people.

Those two sections, at first glance, may seem adequate. Further examination indicates something is lacking. What is lacking is any orientation to the future. The United Methodist ethos is one that is flagrantly open to God's future.

Recently when we were with our family, I was introduced to the amazing world of rockets for children. My granddaughter, Jamie, received a rocket for her birthday. I was fascinated and I helped her put it together. Later, during a weekend when her mom and dad left town, it was an appropriate time to set off the rocket. I seem to get in the most trouble with my grandchildren when their parents leave town!

As I played with the rocket, I discovered a tower that guides the launch. There is the rocket itself and the missile that goes up and carries a parachute for a safe landing. There is an engine that powers the rocket. There is another component, the pad. All these together enable the rocket to be launched. The neighbor children saw what we were doing and two of our grandchildren ran over to be with the neighbors. Soon Jamie came rushing back over to our house. I asked her what she was doing and she said, "I'm going to get my launching pad." She explained that their pad was broken. She ran back over with her launching pad, because what those children had discovered was that the rocket, the engine, and the tower are useless without a good launching pad.

There are three components of the United Methodist ethos which serve as the launching pad which will launch us into God's future.

The first component of the United Methodist ethos which relates to God's future is that United Methodists expect to grow and change.

Time and time again as Jesus talked to his disciples he talked to them with the expectation that they would grow and change, and that where they were "now" was not where they needed to be in the future.

The disciples sensed this expectation when Jesus replied, "But no one puts a piece of unshrunk cloth on an old garment; for the patch pulls away from the garment, and a worse tear results. Nor do men put new wine into old wineskins; otherwise the wineskins burst, and the wine pours out, and the wineskins are ruined; but they put new wine into fresh wineskins, and both are preserved" (Matthew 9:16-17).

All believers affirm that God is the creator. In the Old Testament the word translated "to create" is exclusively used in relationship to God. Human beings do not create, for creation is becoming something out of nothing. This is God's domain. Human beings discover what God has created and is creating. The human quest is one of discovery. This is why human beings are not invited to play God—as if we can create. We are invited to discover. As co-discoverers, United Methodists expect to grow and change.

God's created world is one of change. Our bodies constantly change. With every breath, cells are created as others are sloughed off, no longer needed. Plant and animal life change, climates change. The world is a changing order.

To be relevant the church must change. The church as it was yesterday is not relevant today. In the same way the church as it is today will not be faithful tomorrow. This is difficult to accept.

It is interesting to me to visit with persons who were the architects of changing the church to what it is today, often a relevant serving church, and they feel good about their work. However, at the same time they defend the way the church is and resist change which is required if the church will be faithful to God's changing world in the future.

Is all change good? No

Is all change to be accepted? No

Is change inevitable? Yes. And that is what is clear in the New Testament witness.

Does God author this inevitable change? Yes. This ethos of openness to change is obvious in the polity of The United Methodist Church. The General Conference meets every four years. Because it is a representative body the adopted legislation reflects the change which has already occurred in the life of the church. It is a misunderstanding to have anxiety over this meeting, for General Conference seldom leads the church. Rather, General Conference reflects the change that has already occurred in the church, because this is the way a representative legislative body works. General Conference meets every four years because if the church waits longer the polity is going to be out of date in God's changing world.

This is true in our polity and also in our beliefs. We have historic statements of beliefs but every generation speaks for itself in clarifying the understanding of belief in its generation.

In 1972, The United Methodist Church affirmed the

importance of scripture, tradition, experience and reason in matters of belief. In 1988, another generation re-examined this understanding and placed scripture at an essential location in faith formation in relationship to the other three components of tradition, experience and reason. In 2004 or 2008 another generation will re-examine the 1988 statement to make sure it is relevant as God's changing church in God's changing world.

The only way these changes in belief and polity occur is because of our ethos which allows for change.

United Methodists believe this practice of change is consistent with the biblical witness. When Abraham was called he did not "know it all" to be able to seal the covenant once and for all. Jacob made a discovery about God in struggling with God. Moses made a discovery about the laws of God. Isaiah made a discovery about the work of the people of God as servants. In the New Testament we also discover change. It is interesting to read and study the letters of Paul in the chronological order in which they were written. Paul, when born again on the Road to Damascus, did not "know it all." He continued to discover and change. His last letter, which he sent to the church in Rome, does not represent the same Paul who argued with Peter at the Council of Jerusalem!

The United Methodist ethos is open to discovery. We expect to grow and change! The seven last words of the church, "We have never done it that way" are out of character for United Methodists.

When an acquaintance of mine attended her 35th high school reunion, she went to a small town in Kansas and had a wonderful time. She stayed over Saturday night after the party and decided to attend the little country church where she grew up. She had a marvelous experience. There were five other persons there, including the preacher. She remembered how she had grown up in the faith. At the end of the service, she turned to her seat partner, a person she had sat with 40 years earlier, and said, "This is so won-

derful. It's just the way it used to be." And her seat partner responded, "Honey, it's not wonderful at all. We voted
to close last week."

"Why?"

" Because it's just the way it used to be."

The United Methodist ethos is that we expect to grow
and change!

The hymn, "See How Great a Flame Aspires" by Charles
Wesley states it clearly:

1. "See how great a flame aspires, kindled by a spark of
   grace. Jesus' love the nations fires, sets the kingdoms
   on a blaze. To bring fire on earth he came, kindled in
   some hearts it is; O that all might catch the flame, all
   partake the glorious bliss!

2. When he first the work begun, small and feeble
   was his day; now the Word doth swiftly run, now
   it wins its widening way; more and more it spreads
   and grows, ever mighty to prevail; sin's strongholds it
   now o'erthrows, shakes the trembling gates of hell.

4. Saw ye not the cloud arise, little as a human hand? Now
   it spreads a long the skies, hangs o'er all the thirsty
   land. Lo! The promise of a shower drops already from
   above; but the Lord will shortly pour all the spirit of
   his love."

Questions for Discussion

- Recall an experience in your faith journey when you struggled but felt you had grown greatly. Share that experience with someone.
- Is the understanding that God created a changing world experienced as a threat or an invitation in your life? What about the life of your congregation?
- When in your personal journey of faith were you most confronted with change that was a threat? Share your experiences with someone in your group.
- Consider the changes that have taken place in the life of the church over the last several years. Which ones do you find yourself regretting the most? Why?
- What changes would you like to see in your congregation in the next three to five years that might make it a more attractive, meaningful place to worship and serve?

Chapter 8

United Methodists Join Together Mission And The Evangelistic Task

The second ingredient of our ethos for the future is that mission and the evangelistic task are the inseparable two sides of the same coin and therefore inseparable in our life together.

Many persons affirm that this is a matter of belief and/or polity. I disagree. I think it is a matter of ethic, behavior, of ethos. Behaviorally, we are not called to be schizophrenic, dividing what is one in the gospel of Jesus Christ. Mission and the evangelistic task are one in Christ Jesus.

As Jesus instructed his 12 disciples in Matthew 10, he gave them authority over unclean spirits to cast them out. This is dealing with evil; this has to do with conversion and new life, being born again. On the other hand, to heal every kind of disease and every kind of sickness has to do with mission. In Luke 11 and 19, the stories of the Good Samaritan and Zacchaeus represent the inseparable nature of mission and the evangelistic task. Of course, James stated it so clearly when he wrote, "Even so faith, if it has no works, is dead, being by itself" (2:14-17).

In 1992 during a trip to Angola, I had the privilege of a meeting with the cabinet level Secretary of Culture of that great nation. He was not a Christian. With tears in his eyes he thanked me for the contribution of Methodists to his nation. He said, "Because of your church we have schools and hospitals in Angola. At one time the only schools and hospitals we had were Methodist. Our nation would have no future if it were not for your church. A hundred years ago you came to save souls and save lives. Other African nations," he continued, "are not so fortunate because they did not have Methodist missionaries. They do not have health care and education for all in their nation today. We do because of you."

Friends, the United Methodist life-style—the United Methodist ethos, the character—is one in which mission and the evangelistic task are two sides of the same coin.

Making disciples involves saving souls and saving lives.

When we are in mission, as volunteers or paid staff, and build a building, teach a child, or give a loaf of bread, we are also concerned about and committed to the spiritual journey of those we serve. We must affirm that we do these acts in the name and spirit of Jesus Christ.

To be in mission without evangelistic zeal does not express the United Methodist ethos. On the other hand, to offer a hungry person Christ without giving them food is sinful according to the standards of the life and teachings of Jesus Christ. It is sinful because of the character of Jesus Christ. Jesus Christ was concerned about the spiritual life of the leper, but he also healed the leper because mission and the evangelistic task are two sides of the same coin. Jesus never shared the good news without caring for the physical and mental condition of those who heard. He never cared for the physical and mental condition without sharing the good news. Why? Because mission and evangelistic task are two sides of the same coin.

Friends, in our culture this distinctive piece of our ethos is relevant today. In the whole Christian community, and among United Methodists, there are too many illustrations of the evangelistic task for the sake of numbers and too many illustrations of mission independent of sharing the good news.

For over 200 years, the Methodist movement has been described by historians as the people whose character made us distinctive. Historians have written that the primary reason England did not experience a revolution in the 18th century, as did many nations, including France, was because of John Wesley's Methodist movement, which was represented in the words of the Minister of Culture in Angola, "You save souls and you save lives."

Many of us have been part of emphasizing either mission or the evangelistic task to the neglect of the other. We have sinful camps and parties organized in our denomination around separating the inseparable. We have arguments about which is most important: mission or the evangelical task. This is not a plausible argument if, according to the New Testament, such camps and parties are an expression of sinful corporate life together. This is useless time spent on useless questions trying to separate two sides of the same coin.

Whichever we have done, choosing one rather than the other, or one before the other, we have missed the mark, which is a New Testament description of sin. In Greek, the word for missing the mark is hamartia; when the bull's eye is missed it is called hamartia. Missing the mark is translated "sin." When we emphasize either mission or the evangelistic task to the neglect of the other, we as United Methodists have no distinctive witness and have sinned and fallen short of God's glory!

On the other hand, when we consider both to be two sides of the same coin our witness is distinctive and we are committed to saving souls and lives!

"A Charge to Keep I Have" by Charles Wesley represents this component of our ethos:

1. "A charge to keep I have, a God to glorify,
   a never dying soul to save, and fit it for the sky.
2. To serve the present age, my calling to fulfill;
   O may it all my powers engage to do my Master's will.
3. Arm me with jealous care, as in thy sight to live,
   and oh, thy servant, Lord, prepare a strict account to give!
4. Help me to watch and pray, and on thyself rely,
   assured, if I my trust betray, I shall forever die."

Questions for Discussion

- With which of these two essentials of discipleship—mission or the evangelistic task—are you most comfortable? Why? Share your insights with someone in the group.
- Which would you say is most emphasized in your congregation: mission or evangelism?
- How would you describe the difference between evangelism and membership recruitment? Between missions (sharing the gospel) and doing good?
- What specific steps do you think your church needs to take to balance these twin essentials, mission and evangelism, in the life of your congregation and community?

Chapter 9

United Methodists
Are On The Lookout

The third component of our life-style that provides a pad to launch us into God's future is that United Methodists are always on the lookout. Prior to the modern technology of detection of forest fires by heat sensors, the lookout tower was the key instrument for early detection. Rangers would regularly be on duty to go up on the lookout tower to be on the watch for early signs of fires which could spread into raging destructive events.

The United Methodist life-style and ethos is one in which we are always on the lookout for early signs and indicators both of potential disasters among God's people and indicators of where God is at work.

When I read the New Testament, the Pharisees and Sadducees reflect my own life, for often I want to test Jesus. Matthew 16 describes persons who were testing Jesus, and they asked him to show them a sign from heaven. Jesus answered, "When it is evening, you say, 'It will be fair weather, for the sky is red.' And in the morning, 'There will be a storm today, for the sky is red and threatening.' Do you know how to discern the appearance of the sky, but cannot discern the signs of the times" (Matthew 16:1-3). To discern the signs of the times, we need to be on the lookout tower. We need to be looking around.

This is one of the most disturbing characteristics of the United Methodist ethos. Every United Methodist person, including me, has been concerned sometime because United Methodists have been on the lookout tower. What we see is often disturbing to some of us. Since our practice is to be on the lookout, we deal with issues far earlier than most expressions of the Christian faith.

The Book of Resolutions is the United Methodist record

of what we see from the lookout tower. It's a wonderful resource, written from the perspective of the lookout tower. Historically, which denomination in England saw the sins of child labor and called it the way it was? The Methodists.

Even though it divided the church for a hundred years, which church saw the evils of slavery and named it? The Methodists.

Which denomination dealt with the issues of wholesale discrimination against women, politically, economically and in the church? The Methodists.

Which denomination ten years ago first saw that genetic engineering was being developed in a valueless vacuum and has developed the first contribution of the church in the world to the scientific community in affirming that values, not what is possible, must determine the decisions of scientists in this field of endeavor? The United Methodists. The United Methodist ethic is one in which we take our turns standing on the lookout tower, examining God's world, using an early detection system to identify issues which are affecting the lives of God's children. It is the mandate of the church to deal with these issues.

Certainly, this is a controversial component of our ethos. It makes many United Methodists uneasy to be the first denomination to deal with issues. We become upset with our general agencies and the Council of Bishops, which are mandated by the church to be on the lookout towers for our global and national communities. We see signals and deal with them first. These groups do not speak for the church, but they do speak as a unit of the church which, in our polity, is given the responsibility of standing on the lookout tower and looking at the global and national scene.

Even though they often make us uncomfortable, what would it be like if we did not have these agencies to fulfill this role for us? Often the forest would be ablaze before we were ever warned. And the first words out of our mouths would be, "Why didn't somebody tell us earlier?"

What the general agencies and Council of Bishops do for the global and national scene, every local congregation, institution and agency is called on to do at the local scene. United Methodist members are called to take their turn to survey the scene of the local community to discern early signs of irresponsibility, injustice, and violence, and call the Christian community to faithfulness and responsibility. We are called to detect how God is working outside of the comfortable, cozy walls of the church, and celebrate where God is working in God's world. We are called to be on the lookout for where God is working and to join others in becoming involved as partners with God in our community.

This lookout tower character of our ethos is based on the biblical witness of the prophets in which Jesus called every disciple to discern the signs of the time and be aware of what is happening to God's children which must be addressed.

This lookout tower character of our ethos pulls us into God's future in a way that is thrilling and exciting. We are God's people on the lookout. We are not the front line of defense. The United Methodist ethos is to be God's point person, God's scout, if you will, being where the action is first in the name and spirit of Jesus Christ our Lord.

Questions for Discussion

- In your opinion, is it a good thing for The United Methodist Church to serve as a lookout in today's society, warning us of issues and concerns which affect the lives of God's children? Share your feelings, one way or the other, with the group.
- Are you willing to be on the lookout for the new emerging signals in God's world, or are you more likely to decline that role and take a wait and see attitude toward such concerns? Why?
- Have there been occasions when your local church has led the way and been an early detection system for your community? Make a list of these and discuss them together. What was the result of taking such action?
- Why do you think it is so that in many instances the church is the last place community issues are discussed?
- What concrete steps might be taken to help your congregation become a place where differing ideas, current issues, and sometimes disturbing matters could be openly and thoroughly discussed?

Summary of Section Three:
Launching Into God's Future

In summary, The United Methodist Church will be launched into God's future rather than frozen in the past when three components of our ethos are visible for all to see in every local congregation, agency and institution. United Methodists expect to grow and change, join together mission and the evangelistic task, and are on the lookout.

If a local congregation, agency or institution does not include these components in its life together, atrophy and death will soon be experienced, for what is irrelevant will soon become lifeless. On the other hand, when these components are nourished and celebrated in our life together, The United Methodist Church is an exciting expression of being renewed by God as servant leaders in God's world.

Questions for Discussion

- As a group or with the assistance of a longtime member of your congregation, recall the story of the founding of your congregation. In what ways were the founding persons pulled into God's future or controlled by the past?
- On a scale of one to ten, with ten being exciting and future oriented, and one being "the way it used to be," where would you score your congregation: a) in worship, b) in Sunday School, c) in spiritual growth, d) in mission outreach? List the scores on a sheet of news print and discuss the results.
- As you look at your congregation today, where is it frozen in the past, and where is it moving, being pulled by God's Spirit, into the future?

Conclusion

In conclusion, these nine components of our ethos are what make The United Methodist Church tick, what attracts persons to The United Methodist Church, and what launches us into God's future.

Sometimes The United Methodist Church is as an unwound clock, the pendulum is not moving, the chimes are not ringing on the hour.

Sometimes we are a depolarized magnet. Nothing is being attracted, nothing is being zapped, and no one is being attached.

Sometimes we are like the rocket and engine and tower without a pad.

When this occurs, often our polity and beliefs are in order but we are still stagnant and immovable. On the other hand, United Methodists are alive and growing when we...

1) lead with grace, not judgment;
2) are sent to serve;
3) are committed to ministry with the poor;
4) live in community;
5) experience education without indoctrination;
6) are connected with each other;
7) expect to grow and change;
8) do mission and the evangelistic task together;
9) and are on the lookout for God's activity in the world.

When we are faithful to our United Methodist ethos in these nine ways, our clock is wound; our pendulum is swinging, we are chiming on the hour; we are attracting, zapping and attaching others to our witness. We are launched into God's future because our launching pads are in place; our bells are ringing; we are God's faithful people; and we are singing!

"Love Divine, All Loves Excelling" by Charles

Wesley is an expression of these components:

1. "Love divine, all loves excelling, joy of heaven, to earth come down; fix in us thy humble dwelling; all thy faithful mercies crown! Jesus, thou art all compassion, pure, unbounded love thou art; visit us with thy salvation; enter every trembling heart.

2. Breathe, O breathe thy loving Spirit into every troubled breast! Let us all in thee inherit; let us find that second rest. Take away our bent to sinning; Alpha and Omega be; end of praise thee without ceasing, glory in thy perfect love.

3. Come, Almighty to deliver, let us all thy life receive; suddenly return and never, nevermore thy temples leave. Thee we would be always blessing, serve thee as thy hosts above, pray and praise thee without ceasing, glory in thy perfect love.

4. Finish, then, thy new creation; pure and spotless let us be. Let us see thy great salvation perfectly restored in thee; changed from glory into glory, till in heaven we take our place, till we cast our crowns before thee, lost in wonder, love, and praise."

Discussion Guide
by
*Dr. David Severe

* Dr. Severe is the executive director of the Local Church Ministries Council of the Oklahoma Annual Conference of The United Methodist Church. He has also prepared the discussion questions at the end of each chapter and section.

Discussion Guide
by David L. Severe

It is highly recommended that the video presentation of this material by Bishop Blake be used in conjunction with this book and discussion guide. The communication of feelings, energy and care are much more present in the film than the printed page is able to convey. The video-tape is available through Oklahoma Conference Communications (2420 N. Blackwelder, Okla. City, OK 73106).

Suggestions for the leader of discussion groups:

1. The leader will first want to view the video, read the book and go over all of the questions to have a total vision of the scope of the materials to be covered. Decide how you feel about the questions you will ask, even if you will be (as you should be) very careful of too quickly sharing your opinions.

2. Discussion is best encouraged when people can sit comfortably and can face one another. Arrange seating so that all participants can both see and hear one another clearly.

3. You may wish to ask someone to be the scribe or memory keeper for the group. It is difficult for the leader to lead and keep the record as well. Talk with the person ahead of time and secure their willingness to serve. They will want to be prepared with appropriate note paper, news print, etc., to keep the wisdom of the group intact.

4. As the leader of a discussion group, your task is to facilitate the group more than to inject your own opinions. A good leader will learn to ask the kinds of questions that encourage participants to expand on their statements: *"Where do you see that happening...Give me an example of that."*

5. Good leaders receive *all* contributions of the participants, and just as they offer them. If you are re-

peating what someone has said, never paraphrase! Give back the words as they were spoken. The group will do whatever pushing for clarification, or alteration they think helpful. If the leader does it, the person making a verbal offering feels discounted.

6. A good leader will make sure that all have a chance to participate, not just a few who tend to dominate. Try phrases like: *"Let's hear from someone who has not spoken yet...Does someone over on this side of the circle want to respond to that?...I wonder if someone who has been very quiet up to this point would be willing to share their feelings on this matter?"*

NOTES: